JAMES C. DOBSON, CHARLES R. SWINDOLL,
JAMES MONTGOMERY BOICE, R.C. SPROUL

CHRIST IN CHRISTMAS

A FAMILY ADVENT CELEBRATION

NAVPRESS

A MINISTRY OF THE NAVIGATORS
P.O. BOX 6000, COLORADO SPRINGS, COLORADO 80934

The Navigators is an international Christian organization. Jesus Christ gave His followers the Great Commission to go and make disciples (Matthew 28:19). The aim of The Navigators is to help fulfill that commission by multiplying laborers for Christ in every nation.

NavPress is the publishing ministry of The Navigators. NavPress publications are tools to help Christians grow. Although publications alone cannot make disciples or change lives, they can help believers learn biblical discipleship, and apply what they learn to their lives and ministries.

© 1989 by Ligonier Ministries
All rights reserved, including translation
Library of Congress Catalog Card Number 89-62891
ISBN 08910-96051

Second printing paperback edition, 1990

Cover illustration: Scott Snow
Inside illustrations: Dave Albers (First Sunday of Advent illustration from
    Texas Monthly)

The original concept behind *Christ in Christmas* was developed by Bob Ingram. Some of the material originally appeared in *TableTalk*, a publication produced by Ligonier Ministries, P.O. Box 7500, Orlando, FL 32854. Ligonier, the teaching fellowship of R.C. Sproul, is a national ministry founded to meet the critical needs for substantive adult Christian education.

A portion of "Little Ones to Him Belong" appears in *Let's Make a Memory*, by Gloria Gaither and Shirley Dobson (Waco, Tex.: Word, Inc., 1983), page 60. Used by permission.

"Who Cared About a Jewish Baby Born in Bethlehem!" is from the book *Growing Strong in the Seasons of Life* by Charles R. Swindoll, copyright 1983 by Charles R. Swindoll, Inc., published by Multnomah Press, Portland, Oregon 97266. Used by permission.

"Treasuring Christmas in Our Hearts" is excerpted from the book *The Christ of Christmas* by James Montgomery Boice, copyright 1983 by Moody Bible Institute of Chicago. Used by permission.

The Family Activity sections were prepared by Brian and Frederica Jones, Keene Valley, New York.

Unless otherwise identified, all Scripture quotations are from the *Holy Bible: New International Version* (NIV). Copyright © 1973, 1978, 1984, International Bible Society. Used by permission of Zondervan Bible Publishers. Another version used is the *New King James Version* (NKJV). Copyright © 1979, 1980, 1982, Thomas Nelson Inc., Publishers.

Printed in the United States of America

Contents

Introduction

The celebration of Advent could make this your most memorable Christmas season and be the beginning of a treasured family tradition.

Advent refers to the "coming" or "arrival" of Jesus Christ. Within the Church, the term has several meanings: the Advent of the Lord in the flesh at Christmas; His Advent in Word and Spirit; and the final Advent when our Lord will return bodily in glory. Each meaning stirs the joyful anticipation of what God has accomplished, is doing, and will yet bring to completion.

The purpose of this book is to help busy families find special moments during the Christmas holiday season to ponder and celebrate Christ's advent. A short, home worship experience, which includes carols, Scripture, prayer, and a brief devotional reading, is provided for the four Sundays of Advent, as well as for Christmas Eve. The devotional readings were written by four of today's exceptional Christian communicators—James Boice, James Dobson, R.C. Sproul, and Charles Swindoll.

Daily Bible readings for the entire Advent season are also included. These Scripture excerpts, taken from Genesis to Revelation, reveal clearly the unfolding drama of God's promise, plan, and fulfillment of redemption.

The observance of Advent is something of a late addition to history, as is the celebration of Christmas itself. When the church began to observe Christmas in the fourth century, a period of preparation was added. The length of time varied widely from three to seven weeks.

Not until the tenth century was an agreement reached in the Western world that Advent should consist of four Sundays.

The first Sunday of Advent occurs near or upon November 30. While always including four Sundays, the season may vary in length from twenty-two to twenty-eight days, concluding on Christmas Eve.

A custom that many Christians find meaningful is the preparation of an advent wreath (see the next section "Preparing an Advent Wreath") containing five candles. During each Sunday's observance of Advent, an additional candle is lit. Then on Christmas Eve, all candles, including the fifth in the center of the wreath, are lit. The light burns brightly, providing a fitting climax to the weeks of preparation and symbolically demonstrating the Light of the world that flashed forth centuries ago with the first cry of the Christ child.

Enjoy and celebrate Advent this year! By observing this tradition, the true significance of Christmas will not be missed in your home. May the Light of the world shine brightly in your family this Advent season.

—The Publisher

Preparing an Advent Wreath

For centuries the advent wreath has been made from fresh-cut greenery—pine, laurel, holly, bayberry, or any other evergreen, tree or shrub. Today, an abundance of artificial greenery is available at craft shops and other stores.

The greens are arranged in a circle and four candles are inserted. (A fifth candle—lit on Christmas Eve—is placed in the center of the wreath.) The candles (dripless are best) should be ten inches or longer, since they will be lit on several occasions. The candles may be various colors, although white, purple, or blue are most common.

The making of the wreath can be a family project. One person may buy or gather the greens. Another may construct a form for the greens using wire from coat hangers, for example. Someone else may finally weave the greens together into a circle. The candles can be set in small candlesticks or inserted snugly into the wire frame.

(If you really want to delight the smaller children in your family, candle holders can be formed from clay made with common household ingredients, using the following recipe: Combine three cups of flour, one cup of salt, four ounces of white glue [Elmer's will do], one cup of water, and one teaspoon of lemon juice in a mixing bowl. Stir and knead with hands until ingredients are fully mixed. Divide clay into five portions and place on wax paper or foil. Form your own unique shapes. Place candles in the clay candle holders and *leave in place* until the clay fully hardens. Do not move the candle holders until the clay is dry—normally at least twenty-four hours. After drying, the clay may be painted.)

Place the completed wreath in a location where it has a central focus but will not have to be moved. A dining room table, buffet, counter, hearth, or mantel are possibilities.

Caution must be observed when the candles are lit. *Drying greens can be a serious fire hazard.* Children should be made aware of the potential danger.

Light an additional candle in the advent wreath each week as you gather for your family Advent worship. The soft, flickering light will not only focus your thoughts on the Light of the world, but provide a warm, calming environment in which to prepare your hearts for this year's celebration of Christ's coming.

FIRST SUNDAY OF ADVENT

A CHILD WILL BE BORN TO US

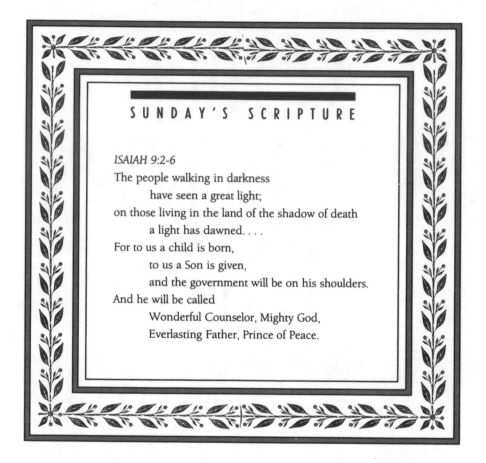

SUNDAY'S SCRIPTURE

ISAIAH 9:2-6
The people walking in darkness
      have seen a great light;
on those living in the land of the shadow of death
      a light has dawned. . . .
For to us a child is born,
      to us a Son is given,
      and the government will be on his shoulders.
And he will be called
      Wonderful Counselor, Mighty God,
      Everlasting Father, Prince of Peace.

AWAY IN A MANGER

Away in a manger, no crib for a bed,
The little Lord Jesus laid down His sweet head.
The stars in the sky looked down where He lay,
The little Lord Jesus, asleep on the hay.

The cattle are lowing, the baby awakes,
The little Lord Jesus, no crying He makes.
I love Thee, Lord Jesus! Look down from the sky,
And stay by my cradle, till morning is nigh.

Be near me, Lord Jesus! I ask Thee to stay
Close by me forever, and love me, I pray.
Bless all the dear children in Thy tender care,
And take us to heaven, to live with Thee there.

Verses 1 and 2, anonymous; Verse 3 by John T. McFarland
James R. Murray, Composer

JAMES C. DOBSON, Ph.D., is founder and president of Focus on the Family, a non-profit organization that produces his nationally syndicated radio program heard daily on more than 1,300 stations.

Dr. Dobson has also been involved in governmental activities. Presidents Carter and Reagan both appointed him to serve on national conferences and task forces, and he also served on the Commission on Pornography.

Dr. Dobson has written nine best-selling books for the family, including *Hide or Seek, The Strong Willed Child, Straight Talk to Men and Their Wives, Love Must be Tough, Love for a Lifetime,* and *Parenting Isn't for Cowards.*

Little Ones to Him Belong

BY JAMES C. DOBSON

less all the dear children in Thy tender care."

I wonder how many of us have ever really thought about these words from the last verse of "Away in a Manger." Sometimes in the flurry of preparing for Christmas, we can easily forget that Advent is a time to prepare our families, especially our children, for the birth of a child that Isaiah said would be called, "Wonderful Counselor, Mighty God, Everlasting Father, Prince of Peace."

If there is any season of the year that seems to summarize all of the enthusiasm, excitement, and wonder of childhood, it is Christmas. I've always loved the Christmas holidays and I suppose I'm still a child in that regard. The toys were exciting and the smell of the Christmas tree still lingers in my mind. When all the family came, the gifts looked like a mountain a mile high to me.

I loved the excitement of relatives arriving and unpacking the car, kids jumping up and down, wrestling, making noise and driving their parents crazy—everything associated with Christmas. And, of course, there was the anticipation, waiting for that big moment to arrive when we opened presents.

But you know, even as a child, there was something much more significant about Christmas than the materialism and presents we shared.

My feelings are very difficult to put into words, but the essence of Christmas had something to do with our family traditions and how those customs affected the people in our family. I'm referring to those family events that are done the same way every year and are anticipated as a time of love, closeness, friendship, and fellowship between family members. These events play an important role not only in preparing a family for Christmas but also in giving it a sense of cohesiveness and stability.

For example, one of the important family traditions in our family centers around food. Each year during Christmas, our family prepares wonderful meals, involving the traditional dishes of turkey, dressing, cranberry sauce, mashed potatoes, and hot rolls that you can smell a block away, and two kinds of salads. We also serve a traditional fruit compote called Ambrosia, which is loved by all of us.

Even though we can hardly walk when we try to leave the table, eating this meal together is a wonderful experience for us. There's a lot of laughter and warm family interaction during these times.

Our traditions aren't limited to the menu alone, of course. During family devotions in Advent, we take the Christmas cards we receive on that day, read them aloud, and pray for the people who sent the cards.

On Christmas Eve, we enjoy a dinner of Chinese food each year. (Don't ask me why. The tradition has simply evolved.) Afterwards, grandparents, aunts, uncles, and cousins join us around the fireplace, and I read from the Bible. After discussing the passages, we lower the lights and my wife, Shirley, gives each member of the family a votive candle. She explains as we take our turn igniting our candle that the light represents Jesus who was born into a dark world to give us eternal life (Isaiah 9:2). As each person lights his candle, he shares one blessing he is especially thankful for during the past year, and something he or she is asking God to do in his life the following year. We then blow out our candles and I close in prayer.

The great value of traditions comes as they give a family a sense of identity, a belongingness. All of us desperately need to feel that we're more than a cluster of people living together in a house; we're a family that is conscious of its personality, character, and heritage, and that our special relationships of love and companionship make us a unit with uniqueness and personality.

By far the most important tradition you can give to your children is to instill deeply ingrained spiritual values in each child. And what better place to start than with the Christmas season.

A very important fringe benefit of Christianity is the tremendous sense of identity that grows out of knowing Jesus Christ. Each is aware, beyond a shadow of a doubt, that he is a personal creation of God. He knows that God knitted him together while in his mother's womb, that the Father now has a plan for his life, and what greater source of self-esteem can there be than to know that Jesus would have died for him if he were the only human being on earth.

Traditions, then, give a family an important sense of identity. A child knows that his home is special and that provides a significant part of his stability as he grows. They help him to know that he too is very special, especially to his Heavenly Father and to His Son, Jesus Christ.

QUESTIONS AND THOUGHTS

1. What Christmas traditions mean the most to you? (Ask this of each person present.)
2. Santa Claus, the buying of gifts, the frantic preparations for the holidays often overshadow the Prince of Peace. During this Christmas season, what can you and others in your family do to make sure that the true meaning of Christmas isn't lost?

WHAT IS NEEDED:
> *One container for each family member (to hold darkness).*
> *One light for each family member (flashlight, candle, lamp, etc.).*

Instruct each member of the family to hold their can of "darkness" and their light. Then turn out all lights in the house. Ask everyone to "walk (a bit) in darkness." Stop when someone gets uncomfortable or enough time has passed to experience darkness. One by one, turn on the lights held by each person.

Reread Isaiah 9 verses 2 and 6. Emphasize the words *light, darkness,* and the names of Jesus.

TALK ABOUT:
1. The problem of darkness. What help was your "can of darkness"? (Note that darkness, in the Bible, is used as a symbol of our lives without Jesus.)
2. What help was your "light"? (Light is a symbol of Jesus and being able to "see.")
3. How much darkness does it take to overcome light?
4. How much light does it take to overcome darkness?

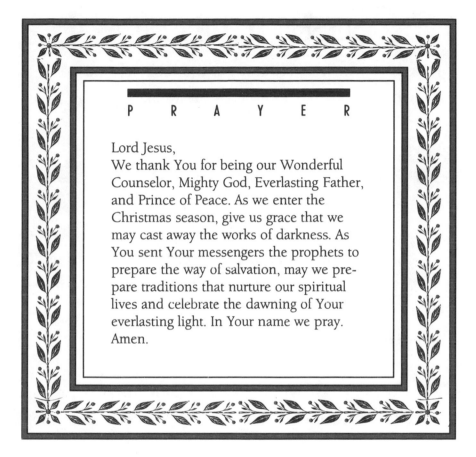

P R A Y E R

Lord Jesus,
We thank You for being our Wonderful
Counselor, Mighty God, Everlasting Father,
and Prince of Peace. As we enter the
Christmas season, give us grace that we
may cast away the works of darkness. As
You sent Your messengers the prophets to
prepare the way of salvation, may we prepare traditions that nurture our spiritual
lives and celebrate the dawning of Your
everlasting light. In Your name we pray.
Amen.

F I R S T   S U N D A Y   O F   A D V E N T

JESUS LOVES ME!

Jesus loves me! this I know, For the Bible tells me so;
Little ones to Him belong, They are weak but He is strong.

REFRAIN

Yes, Jesus loves me! Yes, Jesus loves me!
Yes, Jesus loves me! The Bible tells me so.

Jesus loves me! He who died Heaven's gate to open wide;
He will wash away my sin, Let His little child come in.

REFRAIN

Jesus loves me! He will stay Close beside me all the way;
Thou hast bled and died for me, I will henceforth live for Thee.

REFRAIN

Anna B. Warner, Author
William B. Bradbury, Composer

THE CREATOR OF MAN

GENESIS 1:26-31

T hen God said, "Let us make man in our image, in our likeness, and let them rule over the fish of the sea and the birds of the air, over the livestock, over all the earth, and over all the creatures that move along the ground."

So God created man in his own image, in the image of God he created him; male and female he created them.

God blessed them and said to them, "Be fruitful and increase in number; fill the earth and subdue it. Rule over the fish of the sea and the birds of the air and over every living creature that moves on the ground."

Then God said, "I give you every seed-bearing plant on the face of the whole earth and every tree that has fruit with seed in it. They will be yours for food. And to all the beasts of the earth and all the birds of the air and all the creatures that move on the ground—everything that has the breath of life in it—I give every green plant for food." And it was so.

God saw all that he had made, and it was very good. And there was evening, and there was morning—the sixth day.

THE FALL OF MAN

GENESIS 3:1-24

N ow the serpent was more crafty than any of the wild animals the LORD God had made. He said to the woman, "Did God really say, 'You must not eat from any tree in the garden'?"

The woman said to the serpent, "We may eat fruit from the trees in the garden, but God did say, 'You must not eat fruit from the tree that is in the middle of the garden, and you must not touch it, or you will die.'"

"You will not surely die," the serpent said to the woman. "For God knows that when you eat of it your eyes will be opened, and you will be like God, knowing good and evil."

When the woman saw that the fruit of the tree was good for food and pleasing to the eye, and also desirable for gaining wisdom, she took some and ate it. She also gave some to her husband, who was with her, and he ate it. Then the eyes of both of them were opened, and they realized they were naked; so they sewed fig leaves together and made coverings for themselves.

Then the man and his wife heard the sound of the LORD God as he was walking in the garden in the cool of the day, and they hid from the LORD God among the trees of the garden. But the LORD God called to the man, "Where are you?"

He answered, "I heard you in the garden, and I was afraid because I was naked; so I hid."

And he said, "Who told you that you were naked? Have you eaten from the tree that I commanded you not to eat from?"

The man said, "The woman you put here with me—she gave me some fruit from the tree, and I ate it."

Then the LORD God said to the woman, "What is this you have done?"

The woman said, "The serpent deceived me, and I ate."

So the LORD God said to the serpent, "Because you have done this,

"Cursed are you above all the livestock
      and all the wild animals!
You will crawl on your belly
      and you will eat dust
      all the days of your life.
And I will put enmity
      between you and the woman,
      and between your offspring and hers;
he will crush your head,
      and you will strike his heel."

To the woman he said,

"I will greatly increase your pains in childbearing;
      with pain you will give birth to children.
Your desire will be for your husband,
      and he will rule over you."

To Adam he said, "Because you listened to your wife and ate from the tree about which I commanded you, 'You must not eat of it,'

"Cursed is the ground because of you;
through painful toil you will eat of it
all the days of your life.
It will produce thorns and thistles for you,
and you will eat the plants of the field.
By the sweat of your brow
you will eat your food
until you return to the ground,
since from it you were taken;
for dust you are
and to dust you will return."

Adam named his wife Eve, because she would become the mother of all the living. The LORD God made garments of skin for Adam and his wife and clothed them. And the LORD God said, "The man has now become like one of us, knowing good and evil. He must not be allowed to reach out his hand and take also from the tree of life and eat, and live forever." So the LORD God banished him from the Garden of Eden to work the ground from which he had been taken. After he drove the man out, he placed on the east side of the Garden of Eden cherubim and a flaming sword flashing back and forth to guard the way to the tree of life.

PROMISE OF REDEMPTION

GENESIS 3:15

nd I will put enmity
between you and the woman,
and between your offspring and hers;
he will crush your head,
and you will strike his heel.

A PROPHET WILL COME

DEUTERONOMY 18:15-19

T he LORD your God will raise up for you a prophet like me from among your own brothers. You must listen to him. For this is what you asked of the LORD your God at Horeb on the day of the assembly when you said, "Let us not hear the voice of the LORD our God nor see this great fire anymore, or we will die."

The LORD said to me: "What they say is good. I will raise up for them a prophet like you from among their brothers; I will put my words in his mouth, and he will tell them everything I command him. If anyone does not listen to my words that the prophet speaks in my name, I myself will call him to account."

A VIRGIN WITH CHILD

ISAIAH 7:10-14

 gain the LORD spoke to Ahaz, "Ask the LORD your God for a sign, whether in the deepest depths or in the highest heights."

But Ahaz said, "I will not ask; I will not put the LORD to the test."

Then Isaiah said, "Hear now, you house of David! Is it not enough to try the patience of men? Will you try the patience of my God also? Therefore the Lord himself will give you a sign: The virgin will be with child and will give birth to a son, and will call him Immanuel."

A RIGHTEOUS JUDGE

ISAIAH 11:1-5

A shoot will come up from the stump of Jesse;
  from his roots a Branch will bear fruit.
The Spirit of the LORD will rest on him—
  the Spirit of wisdom and of understanding,
  the Spirit of counsel and of power,
  the Spirit of knowledge and of the fear of the LORD—
and he will delight in the fear of the LORD.

He will not judge by what he sees with his eyes,
  or decide by what he hears with his ears;
but with righteousness he will judge the needy,
  with justice he will give decisions for the poor of the earth.
He will strike the earth with the rod of his mouth;
  with the breath of his lips he will slay the wicked.
Righteousness will be his belt
  and faithfulness the sash around his waist.

THE BIRTH OF CHRIST

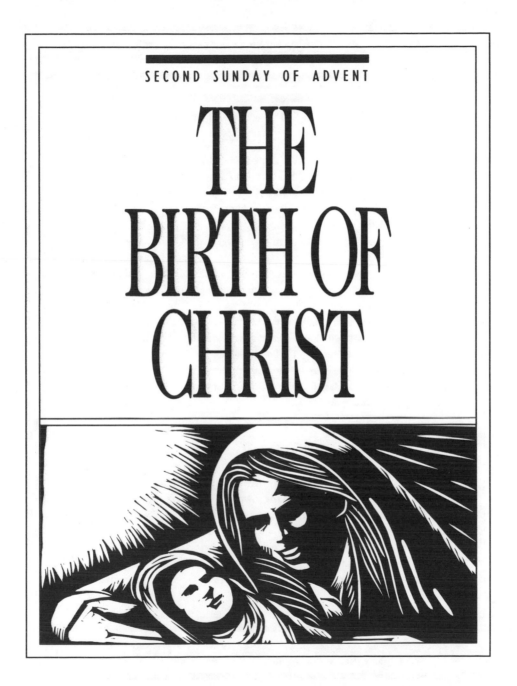

SUNDAY'S SCRIPTURE

MATTHEW 1:18-25

This is how the birth of Jesus Christ came about: His mother Mary was pledged to be married to Joseph, but before they came together, she was found to be with child through the Holy Spirit. Because Joseph her husband was a righteous man and did not want to expose her to public disgrace, he had in mind to divorce her quietly.

But after he had considered this, an angel of the Lord appeared to him in a dream and said, "Joseph son of David, do not be afraid to take Mary home as your wife, because what is conceived in her is from the Holy Spirit. She will give birth to a son, and you are to give him the name Jesus, because he will save his people from their sins."

All this took place to fulfill what the Lord had said through the prophet: "The virgin will be with child and will give birth to a son, and they will call him Immanuel"—which means, "God with us."

When Joseph woke up, he did what the angel of the Lord had commanded him and took Mary home as his wife. But he had no union with her until she gave birth to a son.

LUKE 2:1-7

In those days Caesar Augustus issued a decree that a census should be taken of the entire Roman world. (This was the first census that took place while Quirinius was governor of Syria.) And everyone went to his own town to register.

So Joseph also went up from the town of Nazareth in Galilee to Judea, to Bethlehem the town of David, because he belonged to the house and line of David. He went there to register with Mary, who was pledged to be married to him and was expecting a child. While they were there, the time came for the baby to be born, and she gave birth to her firstborn, a son. She wrapped him in cloths and placed him in a manger, because there was no room for them in the inn.

O LITTLE TOWN OF BETHLEHEM

O little town of Bethlehem, How still we see thee lie!
Above thy deep and dreamless sleep The silent stars go by;
Yet in thy dark streets shineth The everlasting Light:
The hopes and fears of all the years Are met in thee tonight.

For Christ is born of Mary, And gathered all above,
While mortals sleep, the angels keep Their watch of wondering love.
O morning stars, together Proclaim the holy birth!
And praises sing to God the King, And peace to men on earth.

How silently, how silently, The wonderous gift is given!
So God imparts to human hearts The blessings of His Heaven.
No ear may hear His coming, But in this world of sin,
Where meek souls will receive Him still, The dear Christ enters in.

O holy Child of Bethlehem! Descend to us, we pray;
Cast out our sin and enter in, Be born in us today.
We hear the Christmas angels The great glad tidings tell;
O come to us, abide with us, Our Lord Emmanuel!

Phillips Brooks, Author
Lewis H. Redner, Composer

CHARLES R. SWINDOLL is pastor of First Evangelical Free Church in Fullerton, California, and "radio pastor" to Christians around the world through the international broadcasts of "Insight for Living." He is the author of many best-selling books on the Christian life, including: *Growing Strong in the Seasons of Life, Growing Deep in the Christian Life, Come Before Winter, The Quest for Character, Living on the Ragged Edge, Growing Wise in Family Life,* and *Living Beyond the Daily Grind.*

SECOND SUNDAY OF ADVENT

Who Cared About a Jewish Baby Born in Bethlehem!

BY CHARLES R. SWINDOLL

If Dan Rather had been living in 1809, his evening news broadcasts would have concentrated on Austria . . . not Britain or America. The attention of the entire world was on Napoleon as he swept across helpless hamlets like fire across a Kansas wheat field. Nothing else was half as significant on the international scene. The broad brush strokes on the historian's canvas give singular emphasis to the bloody scenes of tyranny created by the diminutive dictator of France. From Trafalgar to Waterloo, his name was a synonym for superiority.

At that time of invasions and battles, babies were being born in Britain and America. But who was interested in babies and bottles, cradles and cribs while history was being made? What could possibly be more important in 1809 than the fall of Austria? Who cared about English-speaking infants that year when Europe was in the limelight?

Somebody should have. A veritable host of thinkers and statesmen drew their first breath in 1809.

☐ *William Gladstone* was born in Liverpool.

☐ *Alfred Tennyson* began his life in Lincolnshire.

☐ *Oliver Wendell Holmes* cried out in Cambridge, Massachusetts.

SECOND SUNDAY OF ADVENT

☐ *Edgar Allan Poe,* a few miles away in Boston, started his brief and tragic life.

☐ A physician named *Darwin* and his wife called their infant son *Charles Robert.*

☐ *Robert Charles Winthrop* wore his first diapers.

☐ A rugged log cabin in Hardin County, Kentucky, owned by an illiterate wandering laborer was filled with the infant screams of a newborn boy named *Abraham Lincoln.*

All that (and more) happened in 1809 . . . but who cared? The destiny of the world was being shaped on battlefields in Austria—*or was it*? No, indeed!

Only a handful of history buffs today could name even one Austrian campaign—but who can measure the impact of those other lives? What appeared to be super-significant to the world has proven to be no more exciting than a Sunday afternoon yawn. What seemed to be totally *insignificant* was, in fact, the genesis of an era.

Go back eighteen centuries before that. Who could have cared about the birth of a baby while the world was watching Rome in all her splendor? Bounded on the west by the Atlantic . . . on the east by the Euphrates . . . on the north by the Rhine and Danube . . . on the south by the Sahara Desert, the Roman Empire was as vast as it was vicious. Political intrigue, racial tension, increased immorality, and enormous military might occupied everyone's attention and conversation. Palestine existed under the crush of Rome's heavy boot. All eyes were on Augustus, the cynical caesar who demanded a census so as to determine a measurement to enlarge taxes. At that time who was interested in a couple making an eighty-mile trip south from Nazareth? What could possibly be more important than Caesar's decisions in Rome? Who cared about a Jewish baby born in Bethlehem?

God did. Without realizing it, mighty Augustus was only an errand boy for the fulfillment of Micah's prediction . . . a pawn in the hand of Jehovah . . . a piece of lint on the pages of prophecy. While Rome was busy making history, God arrived. He pitched His fleshly tent in silence on straw . . . in a stable . . . under a star. The world didn't even notice. Reeling from the wake of Alexander the Great . . . Herod the Great . . . Augustus the Great, the world overlooked Mary's little Lamb.

It still does.

QUESTIONS AND THOUGHTS

1. What was a significant news event the year you were born? (If you don't know, ask your parents or older relatives.)
2. How did the birth of Jesus Christ change the course of history?
3. How did the birth of Jesus Christ change your life?

FAMILY ACTIVITY

WHAT IS NEEDED:
 Paper, pencils, and/or crayons for each family member.

Read Luke 2:1-7 again.

Discuss all the things that might have been going on in and around Bethlehem because of the census and the crowded conditions.

Imagine that you are a reporter for "The Bethlehem Herald" during the census. On your piece of paper draw or illustrate the headlines you would choose for the day *after* Christ was born. When everyone is finished, share these with each other.

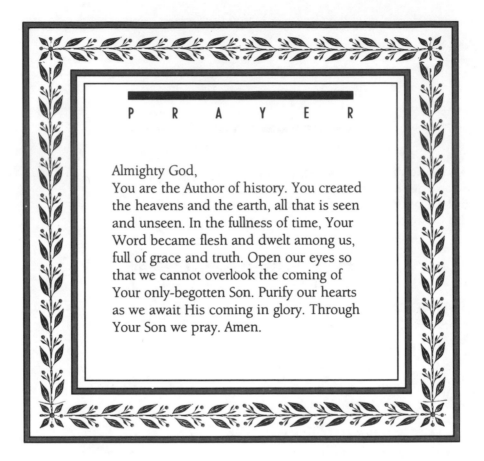

PRAYER

Almighty God,
You are the Author of history. You created
the heavens and the earth, all that is seen
and unseen. In the fullness of time, Your
Word became flesh and dwelt among us,
full of grace and truth. Open our eyes so
that we cannot overlook the coming of
Your only-begotten Son. Purify our hearts
as we await His coming in glory. Through
Your Son we pray. Amen.

SECOND SUNDAY OF ADVENT

O COME, O COME, EMMANUEL

O come, O come, Emmanuel, And ransom captive Israel,
That mourns in lonely exile here, Until the Son of God appear.

REFRAIN

Rejoice! Rejoice! Emmanuel Shall come to thee, O Israel!

O come, Thou Rod of Jesse, free Thine own from Satan's tyranny;
From depths of hell Thy people save And give them victory o'er the grave.

REFRAIN

O come, Thou Dayspring, come and cheer Our spirits by Thine advent here;
And drive away the shades of night, And pierce the clouds and bring us light!

REFRAIN

O come, Thou Key of David, come, And open wide our heavenly home;
Make safe the way that leads on high, And close the path to misery.

REFRAIN

Latin Hymn; John M. Neale, Translator
Thomas Helmore, Composer

A SAVIOR AND DELIVERER

ISAIAH 19:19-25

I n that day there will be an altar to the LORD in the heart of Egypt, and a monument to the LORD at its border. It will be a sign and witness to the LORD Almighty in the land of Egypt. When they cry out to the LORD because of their oppressors, he will send them a savior and defender, and he will rescue them. So the LORD will make himself known to the Egyptians, and in that day they will acknowledge the LORD. They will worship with sacrifices and grain offerings; they will make vows to the LORD and keep them. The LORD will strike them and heal them. They will turn to the LORD, and he will respond to their pleas and heal them.

In that day there will be a highway from Egypt to Assyria. The Assyrians will go to Egypt and the Egyptians to Assyria. The Egyptians and Assyrians will worship together. In that day Israel will be the third, along with Egypt and Assyria, a blessing on the earth. The LORD Almighty will bless them, saying "Blessed be Egypt my people, Assyria my handiwork, and Israel my inheritance."

THE SOVEREIGN LORD COMES

ISAIAH 40:9-11

Y ou who bring good tidings to Zion,
    go up on a high mountain.
You who bring good tidings to Jerusalem,
    lift up your voice with a shout,
lift it up, do not be afraid;
    say to the towns of Judah,
    "Here is your God!"
See, the Sovereign LORD comes with power,
    and his arm rules for him.

See, his reward is with him,
    and his recompense accompanies him.
He tends his flock like a shepherd:
    He gathers the lambs in his arms
and carries them close to his heart;
    he gently leads those that have young.

BEHOLD MY CHOSEN ONE

ISAIAH 42:1-4

ere is my servant, whom I uphold,
    my chosen one in whom I delight;
I will put my Spirit on him
    and he will bring justice to the nations.
He will not shout or cry out,
    or raise his voice in the streets.
A bruised reed he will not break,
    and a smoldering wick he will not snuff out.
In faithfulness he will bring forth justice;
    he will not falter or be discouraged
till he establishes justice on earth.
    In his law the islands will put their hope."

A SERVANT BRINGS SALVATION

ISAIAH 49:1-7

isten to me, you islands;
    hear this you distant nations:
Before I was born the LORD called me;

from my birth he has made mention of my name.
He made my mouth like a sharpened sword,
    in the shadow of his hand he hid me;
he made me into a polished arrow
    and concealed me in his quiver.
He said to me, "You are my servant,
    Israel, in whom I will display my splendor."
But I said, "I have labored to no purpose;
    I have spent my strength in vain and for nothing.
Yet what is due me is in the LORD's hand,
    and my reward is with my God."

And now the LORD says—
    he who formed me in the womb to be his servant
to bring Jacob back to him
    and gather Israel to himself,
for I am honored in the eyes of the LORD
    and my God has been my strength—
he says:
"It is too small a thing for you to be my servant
    to restore the tribes of Jacob
    and bring back those of Israel I have kept.
I will also make you a light for the Gentiles,
    that you may bring my salvation to the ends of the earth."

This is what the LORD says—
    the Redeemer and Holy One of Israel—
to him who was despised and abhorred by the nation,
    to the servant of rulers:
"Kings will see you and arise,
    princes will see and bow down,
because of the LORD, who is faithful,
    the Holy One of Israel, who has chosen you."

A MAN OF SORROWS

ISAIAH 53:1-12

W ho has believed our message
        and to whom has the arm of the LORD been revealed?
He grew up before him like a tender shoot,
        and like a root out of dry ground.
He had no beauty or majesty to attract us to him,
        nothing in his appearance that we should desire him.
He was despised and rejected by men,
        a man of sorrows, and familiar with suffering.
Like one from whom men hide their faces
        he was despised, and we esteemed him not.

Surely he took up our infirmities
        and carried our sorrows,
yet we considered him stricken by God,
        smitten by him, and afflicted.
But he was pierced for our transgressions,
        he was crushed for our iniquities;
the punishment that brought us peace was upon him,
        and by his wounds we are healed.
We all, like sheep, have gone astray,
        each of us has turned to his own way;
and the LORD has laid on him
        the iniquity of us all.

He was oppressed and afflicted,
        yet he did not open his mouth;
he was led like a lamb to the slaughter,
        and as a sheep before her shearers is silent,
        so he did not open his mouth.
By oppression and judgment, he was taken away.
        And who can speak of his descendants?

For he was cut off from the land of the living;
    for the transgressions of my people he was stricken.
He was assigned a grave with the wicked,
    and with the rich in his death,
though he had done no violence,
    nor was any deceit in his mouth.

Yet it was the LORD's will to crush him and cause him to suffer,
    and though the LORD makes his life a guilt offering,
he will see his offspring and prolong his days,
    and the will of the LORD will prosper in his hand.
After the suffering of his soul,
    he will see the light of life and be satisfied;
by his knowledge my righteous servant will justify many,
    and he will bear their iniquities.
Therefore I will give him a portion among the great,
    and he will divide the spoils with the strong,
because he poured out his life unto death,
    and was numbered with the transgressors.
For he bore the sin of many,
    and made intercession for the transgressors.

SATURDAY'S SCRIPTURE READING

GOD'S SPIRIT IS UPON HIM

ISAIAH 61:1-3

T he Spirit of the Sovereign LORD is on me,
    because the LORD has anointed me
    to preach good news to the poor.
He has sent me to bind up the brokenhearted,
    to proclaim freedom for the captives
    and release for the prisoners,
to proclaim the year of the LORD's favor
    and the day of vengeance of our God,

S E C O N D   W E E K   O F   A D V E N T

to comfort all who mourn,
　　　and provide for those who grieve in Zion—
to bestow on them a crown of beauty
　　　instead of ashes,
the oil of gladness
　　　instead of mourning,
and a garment of praise
　　　instead of a spirit of despair.
They will be called oaks of righteousness,
　　　a planting of the LORD
　　　for the display of his splendor.

THE SHEPHERDS & THE ANGELS

LUKE 2:8-20

And there were shepherds living out in the fields nearby, keeping watch over their flocks at night. An angel of the Lord appeared to them, and the glory of the Lord shone around them, and they were terrified. But the angel said to them, "Do not be afraid. I bring you good news of great joy that will be for all the people. Today in the town of David a Savior has been born to you; he is Christ the Lord. This will be a sign to you: You will find a baby wrapped in cloths and lying in a manger."

Suddenly a great company of the heavenly host appeared with the angel, praising God and saying,

"Glory to God in the highest,
          and on earth peace to men on whom his favor rests."

When the angels had left them and gone into heaven, the shepherds said to one another, "Let's go to Bethlehem and see this thing that has happened, which the Lord has told us about."

So they hurried off and found Mary and Joseph, and the baby, who was lying in the manger. When they had seen him, they spread the word concerning what had been told them about this child, and all who heard it were amazed at what the shepherds said to them. But Mary treasured up all these things and pondered them in her heart. The shepherds returned, glorifying and praising God for all the things they had heard and seen, which were just as they had been told.

SILENT NIGHT, HOLY NIGHT

Silent night, holy night, All is calm, all is bright
Round yon virgin mother and child! Holy Infant so tender and mild,
Sleep in heavenly peace, Sleep in heavenly peace.

Silent night, holy night, Shepherds quake at the sight.
Glories stream from heaven afar, Heavenly hosts sing Alleluia;
Christ the Savior, is born! Christ, the Savior, is born.

Silent night, holy night, Son of God, love's pure light
Radiant beams from Thy holy face, With the dawn of redeeming grace,
Jesus, Lord, at Thy birth, Jesus, Lord, at Thy birth.

Joseph Mohr, Author
Franz Gruber, Composer

JAMES MONTGOMERY BOICE (B.A., Harvard University; B.D., Princeton Theological Seminary; Th.D., University of Basel, Switzerland) is the speaker on the worldwide radio ministry of "The Bible Study Hour" and pastor of historic Tenth Presbyterian Church, Philadelphia, founded in 1828. He is also the chairman of the International Council on Biblical Inerrancy and founder of the Philadelphia Conference on Reformed Theology.

Dr. Boice's twenty-five book and video cassette titles include *The Gospel of John* (five volumes), *How to Live the Christian Life, Getting to Know God, The Sermon on the Mount, The Parables of Jesus, Foundations of the Christian Faith* (four volumes), and *The Christ of Christmas*.

Treasuring Christmas in Our Hearts

BY JAMES MONTGOMERY BOICE

ow should we celebrate Christmas?

If you are not a Christian, the best way to celebrate Christmas is by becoming a Christian, that is, by believing in Jesus, asking Him to come into your heart and determining to follow Him as His disciple. But perhaps you already are a Christian. Perhaps you already have believed in Jesus. How should you celebrate Christmas then?

The story of Mary and the shepherds and the angels gives us some clues.

First, the shepherds "spread the word concerning what had been told them about this child" (Luke 2:17). This means that they became witnesses to Jesus. That God used them to spread this heavenly message must have stunned them. Shepherds were a despised class in first-century Palestine. The nature of their calling kept them from observing the ceremonial law, which meant a lot to religious people. Shepherds were also considered unreliable and were not even allowed to give testimony in the law courts.

But the angels came to shepherds with the great message that Christ the Lord—the Savior of the world—had been born in the town of David. And despite what others thought of them, the shepherds knew that lost people needed to hear that great message. It is the same today. Jesus is the world's Savior. And people are still lost without Him.

Second, the people who heard the message "were amazed at what the shepherds said to them" (verse 18). People today are hardly amazed at anything, but it is hard to see how anyone can understand what Christmas is about and not be amazed. Christmas is the story of God becoming a man, like us, in order to save us from our sins. This truth was so astonishing that people believed even shepherds! But aren't you amazed when you think about what God did for us? Yes, there is much about God becoming man that we cannot understand, but even if we could understand every bit of it, we still would be amazed.

Third, Mary "treasured up all these things and pondered them in her heart" (verse 19). What Mary did went beyond mere amazement, though she marveled too. This wonderful woman also made an attempt to remember everything that was happening to her in those days and then to figure out what each of these things meant. That is, she took time to think about spiritual things, just as we should do. Christmas is a very busy time. But our time is badly spent if we allow the business of Christmas to keep us from reading the Christmas story again and again, and thinking about it.

Fourth, the shepherds "returned glorifying and praising God for all the things they had heard and seen" (verse 20). This means that they spoke not just to others about the birth of Jesus. They also spoke to God, praising Him for it. They saw the birth of Jesus as something God had done, and they wanted to thank Him.

Here's a suggestion. If you are willing to try to celebrate Christmas like Mary and the shepherds did, don't begin with verse 17, which tells us to tell others about Jesus. Begin with verses 18-20, which tell us to wonder at the birth of Jesus, to ponder its meaning, and to praise God for it. Praise God for sending Jesus. Think about why Jesus came to earth on that cold night so long ago. And marvel that, because of His birth, life, death, and resurrection, you have not suffered God's just punishment for your sins but rather have been saved from them.

When you have really thought about these things and thanked God for them, go back to verse 17 and tell others, as the shepherds did. And last, think about what you can give back to the Lord for this amazing gift.

QUESTIONS AND THOUGHTS

1. What are some of the things that amaze you most about the Christmas story?
2. If someone said to you, "Tell me why God sent Jesus to earth," what would you say?
3. Can you think of anyone you know who needs to be told the amazing story of Christmas? How could you do this during this Advent season?

FAMILY ACTIVITY

WHAT IS NEEDED:
    Paper, pencils, and/or crayons for each family member.

Discuss what it means to be amazed (see Luke 2:8-20, especially verse 18). How is being amazed different from fear?

Ask each person to list things that he or she finds amazing. (Younger children will need help with the writing but give them time to think this out for themselves.) Share your ideas with each other.

Write your own short psalm of praise (just two or three sentences), or create a drawing that expresses praise to the Lord. Share with the others.

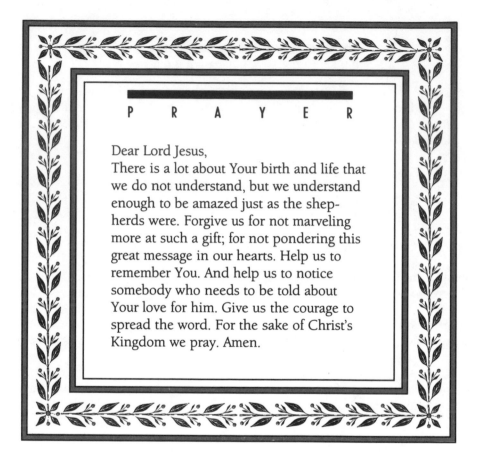

P R A Y E R

Dear Lord Jesus,
There is a lot about Your birth and life that
we do not understand, but we understand
enough to be amazed just as the shepherds were. Forgive us for not marveling
more at such a gift; for not pondering this
great message in our hearts. Help us to
remember You. And help us to notice
somebody who needs to be told about
Your love for him. Give us the courage to
spread the word. For the sake of Christ's
Kingdom we pray. Amen.

T H I R D   S U N D A Y   O F   A D V E N T

O COME, ALL YE FAITHFUL

O come, all ye faithful, joyful and triumphant,
O come ye, o come ye to Bethlehem;
Come and behold Him, born the King of angels;

REFRAIN
O come, let us adore Him, O come, let us adore Him,
O come, let us adore Him, Christ, the Lord.

Sing, choirs of angels, sing in exultation,
O sing all ye citizens of heaven above;
Glory to God, all glory in the highest;

REFRAIN

Yea, Lord, we greet Thee, born this happy morning,
O Jesus, to Thee be all glory given;
Word of the Father, now in flesh appearing;

REFRAIN

Latin Hymn; Frederick Oakeley, Translator
From John F. Wade's Cantus Diversi

A RIGHTEOUS BRANCH

JEREMIAH 23:5-6

T he days are coming," declares the LORD,
  "when I will raise up to David a righteous Branch,
a King who will reign wisely
  and do what is just and right in the land.
In his days Judah will be saved
  and Israel will live in safety.
This is the name by which he will be called:
  The LORD Our Righteousness.

A RULER OVER ISRAEL

MICAH 5:2

B ut you, Bethlehem Ephrathah,
  though you are small among the clans of Judah,
out of you will come for me
  one who will be ruler over Israel,
whose origins are from of old,
  from ancient times.

YOUR KING IS COMING

ZECHARIAH 9:9-10

R ejoice greatly, O Daughter of Zion!
        Shout, daughter of Jerusalem!
See, your king comes to you,
        righteous and having salvation,
        gentle and riding on a donkey,
        on a colt, the foal of a donkey.
I will take away the chariots from Ephraim
        and the war-horses from Jerusalem,
        and the battle bow will be broken.
He will proclaim peace to the nations.
        His rule will extend from sea to sea
        and from the River to the ends of the earth.

THE MESSENGER IS SENT

MALACHI 3:1

S ee, I will send my messenger, who will prepare the way before me. Then suddenly the Lord you are seeking will come to his temple; the messenger of the covenant, whom you desire, will come," says the LORD Almighty.

THE BIRTH OF JOHN IS FORETOLD

LUKE 1:1-25

Many have undertaken to draw up an account of the things that have been fulfilled among us, just as they were handed down to us by those who from the first were eyewitnesses and servants of the word. Therefore, since I myself have carefully investigated everything from the beginning, it seemed good also to me to write an orderly account for you, most excellent Theophilus, so that you may know the certainty of the things you have been taught.

In the time of Herod king of Judea there was a priest named Zechariah, who belonged to the priestly division of Abijah; his wife Elizabeth was also a descendant of Aaron. Both of them were upright in the sight of God, observing all the Lord's commandments and regulations blamelessly. But they had no children, because Elizabeth was barren; and they were both well along in years.

Once when Zechariah's division was on duty and he was serving as priest before God, he was chosen by lot, according to the custom of the priesthood to go into the temple of the Lord and burn incense. And when the time for the burning of incense came, all the assembled worshipers were praying outside.

Then an angel of the Lord appeared to him, standing at the right side of the altar of incense. When Zechariah saw him, he was startled and was gripped with fear. But the angel said to him: "Do not be afraid, Zechariah; your prayer has been heard. Your wife Elizabeth will bear you a son, and you are to give him the name John. He will be a joy and delight to you, and many will rejoice because of his birth, for he will be great in the sight of the Lord. He is never to take wine or other fermented drink, and he will be filled with the Holy Spirit even from birth. Many of the people of Israel will he bring back to the Lord their God. And he will go on before the Lord, in the spirit and power of Elijah, to turn the hearts of the fathers to their children and the disobedient to the wisdom of the righteous—to make ready a people prepared for the Lord."

Zechariah asked the angel, "How can I be sure of this? I am an old man and my wife is well along in years."

The angel answered, "I am Gabriel. I stand in the presence of God, and I have been sent to speak to you and to tell you this good news. And now you will be silent and not able to speak until the day this happens, because you did not believe my words, which will come true at their proper time."

Meanwhile, the people were waiting for Zechariah and wondering why he stayed so long in the temple. When he came out, he could not speak to them. They realized he had seen a vision in the temple, for he kept making signs to them but remained unable to speak.

When his time of service was completed, he returned home. After this his wife Elizabeth became pregnant and for five months remained in seclusion. "The Lord has done this for me," she said. "In these days he has shown his favor and taken away my disgrace among the people."

THE ANNOUNCEMENT TO MARY

LUKE 1:26-38

In the sixth month, God sent the angel Gabriel to Nazareth, a town in Galilee, to a virgin pledged to be married to a man named Joseph, a descendant of David. The virgin's name was Mary. The angel went to her and said, "Greetings, you who are highly favored! The Lord is with you."

Mary was greatly troubled at his words and wondered what kind of greeting this might be. But the angel said to her, "Do not be afraid, Mary, you have found favor with God. You will be with child and give birth to a son, and you are to give him the name Jesus. He will be great and will be called the Son of the Most High. The Lord God will give him the throne of his father David, and he will reign over the house of Jacob forever; his kingdom will never end."

"How will this be," Mary asked the angel, "since I am a virgin?"

The angel answered, "The Holy Spirit will come upon you, and the power of the Most High will overshadow you. So the holy one to be born will be called the Son of God. Even Elizabeth your relative is going to have a child in her old age, and she who was said to be barren is in her sixth month. For nothing is impossible with God."

"I am the Lord's servant," Mary answered. "May it be to me as you have said." Then the angel left her.

THE VISIT OF THE MAGI

MATTHEW 2:1-12

After Jesus was born in Bethlehem in Judea, during the time of King Herod, Magi from the east came to Jerusalem and asked, "Where is the one who has been born king of the Jews? We saw his star in the east and have come to worship him."

When King Herod heard this he was disturbed, and all Jerusalem with him. When he had called together all the people's chief priests and teachers of the law, he asked them where the Christ was to be born. "In Bethlehem in Judea," they replied, "for this is what the prophet has written:

"'But you, Bethlehem, in the land of Judah,
    are by no means least among the rulers of Judah;
for out of you will come a ruler
    who will be the shepherd of my people Israel.'"

Then Herod called the Magi secretly and found out from them the exact time the star had appeared. He sent them to Bethlehem and said, "Go and make a careful search for the child. As soon as you find him, report to me, so that I too may go and worship him."

After they had heard the king, they went on their way, and the star they had seen in the east went ahead of them until it stopped over the place where the child was. When they saw the star, they were overjoyed. On coming to the house, they saw the child with his mother Mary, and they bowed down and worshiped him. Then they opened their treasures and presented him with gifts of gold and of incense and of myrrh. And having been warned in a dream not to go back to Herod, they returned to their country by another route.

WE THREE KINGS

We three kings of Orient are, Bearing gifts we traverse afar
Field and fountain, moor and mountain, Following yonder star.

REFRAIN
O star of wonder, star of night, Star with royal beauty bright,
Westward leading, still proceeding, Guide us to Thy perfect light.

Born a King on Bethlehem's plain, Gold I bring to crown Him again,
King forever, ceasing never Over us all to reign.

REFRAIN

Frankincense to offer have I, Incense owns a Deity nigh;
Prayer and praising all men raising, Worship Him, God on high.

REFRAIN

Myrrh is mine, its bitter perfume Breathes a life of gathering gloom:
Sorrowing, sighing, bleeding, dying, Sealed in the stone-cold tomb.

REFRAIN

Glorious now behold Him arise, King and God and Sacrifice;
Alleluia, Alleluia! Sounds through the earth and skies.

REFRAIN

John Hopkins, Author and Composer

DR. R.C. SPROUL, a nationally recognized theologian, is known for his ability to communicate deep truths in a fresh and easy-to-understand style. The chairman of Ligonier Ministries in Orlando, Florida, which provides biblical instruction for laypersons, Dr. Sproul is currently professor of systematic theology and apologetics at Reformed Theological Seminary. He lectures nationwide and has an extensive audio and video tape teaching ministry. Dr. Sproul is the author of twenty-one books, including *The Holiness of God, Knowing Scripture, Reason to Believe,* and *One Holy Passion.*

FOURTH SUNDAY OF ADVENT

The Big King and the Little King

BY R.C. SPROUL

nce upon a time, in the tiny land of Palestine, two kings were alive at the same time and at the same place. One of the kings was about seventy years old; the other king was an infant. The big king was evil; the little king was pure. The big king was rich and powerful; the little king was stricken by poverty. The big king lived in an opulent palace; the little king lived in a stable. The little king's mother was a peasant girl; His adoptive father was a carpenter.

The big king's name was Herod. He was called "The Great." He was a "puppet-king." That is, in this period of Jewish history, Palestine was ruled by the emperor of Rome. Rome had conquered Palestine in war and the emperor had placed a local fellow in Galilee to be his deputy there. Herod became governor of Galilee in 40 BC, and in the same year the Roman Senate declared him "King of Judea."

Herod was a master builder. He is famous for building a magnificent temple in Jerusalem. One wall of that temple, the Wailing Wall, still stands, boasting the giant stones that were King Herod's trademark.

But Herod had a problem. Though he was called "King of Judea," he could not be a true king of the Jews. He was not of the tribe of Judah. He was not a descendant of David. He was not even a Jew.

One day Herod received some unusual visitors. They were men from the East. Tradition calls them three kings, but they were really magi or astrologers, possibly from Persia. The magi came to Herod because they were following a star that led them to Palestine. They inquired of Herod, "Where is He who has been born King of the Jews? For we have seen His star in the East and have come to worship Him."

Herod was greatly troubled by the question. He didn't like the idea of another king in his realm, especially a true king who was annointed by God. He tried to fool the wise men. He met with them secretly and asked them how to find this newborn king. He lied to the magi. He pretended to want to find the baby king so he could worship Him. What he really wanted was to kill the little king.

The magi left King Herod and followed the star to Bethlehem where they found the baby king. They fell down and worshiped Him. They presented gifts to Him. These gifts were uncommon. They were the type of gifts that in the Old Testament were reserved for royalty. They were gifts of gold, frankincense, and myrrh.

When Herod realized that the magi fooled him he became enraged. He commanded all the male babies two years old and under, who lived in and around Bethlehem, to be killed.

But God warned the baby king's father, who fled with his wife and baby to Egypt. In a short time King Herod died and the new king and His parents came back to Palestine.

The big king died and now is remembered as a little king. The little king grew up and became Jesus the Greatest. He is now the King of all the kings and the Lord of all the lords.

This simple story is a tragic footnote to the first Christmas. It is the record of a king who missed his King. In the world and in history there have been many kings, queens, princes, and princesses. Each of them has ruled with limited sovereignty. Yet each of these persons who has ever worn a crown has been under the dominion and authority of the Supreme King. Christmas marks the birthdate of ultimate royalty, the nativity of the superlative King, the King of all the kings who reigns forever.

QUESTIONS AND THOUGHTS

1. Why was King Herod so afraid of the baby Jesus?
2. What makes this story of how Herod "missed his King" so tragic? How can it still be tragic today?
3. How do we try to remove Jesus' authority from our lives today?

FAMILY ACTIVITY

WHAT IS NEEDED:
   Paper bags for puppets (at least three: King Herod, one Magi, and the Chief Priest).
   Crayons.
   Sticks or pencils to support the puppets.
   Newspaper to stuff the puppets.
   Tape to attach puppets to sticks.
OR
   Use only the crayons and bag—working the puppet with your hand, using the fold in the bag as the puppet's mouth.

Explain to the children that they will be making puppets based on the persons in today's Scripture reading (Matthew 2:1-12). If necessary, review the passage and help children select their puppet character.

THE ACTING OUT CAN BE DONE IN ONE OF TWO WAYS:
   Have some of the family write the script and read it while the puppet makers act out the dialogue with their puppets.
OR
   Have everyone work on a puppet and each character make up the dialogue as the story is acted out.

Discuss the difference between an expectant heart and a jealous heart.

FOURTH SUNDAY OF ADVENT

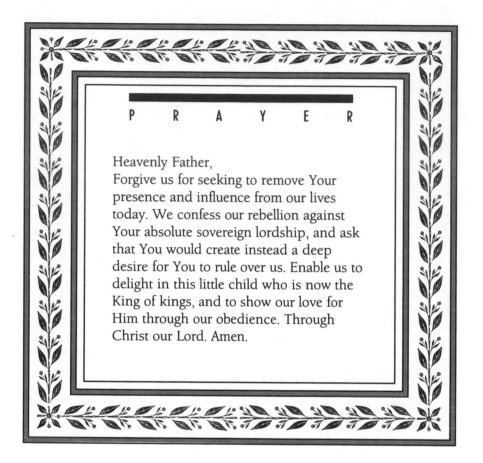

PRAYER

Heavenly Father,
Forgive us for seeking to remove Your
presence and influence from our lives
today. We confess our rebellion against
Your absolute sovereign lordship, and ask
that You would create instead a deep
desire for You to rule over us. Enable us to
delight in this little child who is now the
King of kings, and to show our love for
Him through our obedience. Through
Christ our Lord. Amen.

FOURTH SUNDAY OF ADVENT

THE FIRST NOEL

The first noel the angel did say
Was to certain poor shepherds in fields as they lay—
In fields where they lay keeping their sheep,
On a cold winter's night that was so deep.

REFRAIN
Noel, noel! Noel, noel!
Born is the King of Israel!

They looked up and saw a star
Shining in the east, beyond them far;
And to the earth it gave great light,
And so it continued both day and night.

REFRAIN

And by the light of that same star,
Three Wise Men came from country far;
To seek for a king was their intent,
And to follow the star wherever it went.

REFRAIN

Then let us all with one accord
Sing praises to our heavenly Lord,
That hath made heaven and earth of naught,
And with His blood mankind hath bought.

REFRAIN

English Carol, before 1823; Traditional Melody
From Sandys' "Christmas Carols," 1833

ELIZABETH AND MARY

LUKE 1:39-56

At that time Mary got ready and hurried to a town in the hill country of Judah, where she entered Zechariah's home and greeted Elizabeth. When Elizabeth heard Mary's greeting, the baby leaped in her womb, and Elizabeth was filled with the Holy Spirit. In a loud voice she exclaimed: "Blessed are you among women, and blessed is the child you will bear! But why am I so favored, that the mother of my Lord should come to me? As soon as the sound of your greeting reached my ears, the baby in my womb leaped for joy. Blessed is she who has believed that what the Lord has said to her will be accomplished!"

And Mary said:

"My soul praises the Lord
      and my spirit rejoices in God my Savior,
for he has been mindful of the humble state of his servant.
From now on all generations will call me blessed,
      for the Mighty One has done great things for me—
      holy is his name.
His mercy extends to those who fear him,
      from generation to generation.
He has performed mighty deeds with his arm;
      he has scattered those who are proud in their inmost thoughts.
He has brought down rulers from their thrones
      but has lifted up the humble.
He has filled the hungry with good things
      but has sent the rich away empty.
He has helped his servant Israel,
      remembering to be merciful
to Abraham and his descendants forever,
      even as he said to our fathers."

Mary stayed with Elizabeth for about three months and then returned home.

THE BIRTH OF JESUS

LUKE 2:1-20

In those days Caesar Augustus issued a decree that a census should be taken of the entire Roman world. (This was the first census that took place while Quirinius was governor of Syria.) And everyone went to his own town to register.

So Joseph also went up from the town of Nazareth in Galilee to Judea, to Bethlehem the town of David, because he belonged to the house and line of David. He went there to register with Mary, who was pledged to be married to him and was expecting a child. While they were there, the time came for the baby to be born, and she gave birth to her firstborn, a son. She wrapped him in cloths and placed him in a manger, because there was no room for them in the inn.

And there were shepherds living out in the fields nearby, keeping watch over their flocks at night. An angel of the Lord appeared to them, and the glory of the Lord shone around them, and they were terrified. But the angel said to them, "Do not be afraid. I bring you good news of great joy that will be for all the people. Today in the town of David a Savior has been born to you; he is Christ the Lord. This will be a sign to you: You will find a baby wrapped in cloths and lying in a manger."

Suddenly a great company of the heavenly host appeared with the angel, praising God and saying,

"Glory to God in the highest,
and on earth peace to men on whom his favor rests."

When the angels had left them and gone into heaven, the shepherds said to one another, "Let's go to Bethlehem and see this thing that has happened, which the Lord has told us about."

So they hurried off and found Mary and Joseph, and the baby, who was lying in the manger. When they had seen him, they spread the word concerning what had been told them about this child, and all who heard it were amazed at what the shepherds said to them. But Mary treasured up all these things and pondered them in her heart. The shepherds returned, glorifying and praising God for all the things they had heard and seen, which were just as they had been told.

PRESENTATION IN THE TEMPLE

LUKE 2:21-38

O n the eighth day, when it was time to circumcise him, he was named Jesus, the name the angel had given him before he had been conceived.

When the time of their purification according to the Law of Moses had been completed, Joseph and Mary took him to Jerusalem to present him to the Lord (as it is written in the Law of the Lord, "Every firstborn male is to be consecrated to the Lord"), and to offer a sacrifice in keeping with what is said in the Law of the Lord: "a pair of doves or two young pigeons."

Now there was a man in Jerusalem called Simeon, who was righteous and devout. He was waiting for the consolation of Israel, and the Holy Spirit was upon him. It had been revealed to him by the Holy Spirit that he would not die before he had seen the Lord's Christ. Moved by the Spirit, he went into the temple courts. When the parents brought in the child Jesus to do for him what the custom of the Law required, Simeon took him in his arms and praised God, saying:

> "Sovereign Lord, as you have promised,
>   you now dismiss your servant in peace.
> For my eyes have seen your salvation,
>   which you have prepared in the sight of all people,
> a light for revelation to the Gentiles
>   and for glory to your people Israel."

The child's father and mother marveled at what was said about him. Then Simeon blessed them and said to Mary, his mother: "This child is destined to cause the falling and rising of many in Israel, and to be a sign that will be spoken against, so that the thoughts of many hearts will be revealed. And a sword will pierce your own soul too."

There was also a prophetess, Anna, the daughter of Phanuel, of the tribe of Asher. She was very old; she had lived with her husband seven years after her marriage, and then was a widow until she was eighty-four. She never left the temple but worshiped night and day, fasting and praying. Coming up to them at that very moment, she gave thanks to God and spoke about the child to all who were looking forward to the redemption of Jerusalem.

THE PRE-EMINENT CHRIST

COLOSSIANS 1:15-23

He is the image of the invisible God, the firstborn over all creation. For by him all things were created: things in heaven and on earth, visible and invisible, whether thrones or powers or rulers or authorities; all things were created by him and for him. He is before all things, and in him all things hold together. And he is the head of the body, the church; he is the beginning and the firstborn from among the dead, so that in everything he might have the supremacy. For God was pleased to have all his fullness dwell in him, and through him to reconcile to himself all things, whether things on earth or things in heaven, by making peace through his blood, shed on the cross.

Once you were alienated from God and were enemies in your minds because of your evil behavior. But now he has reconciled you by Christ's physical body through death to present you holy in his sight, without blemish and free from accusation—if you continue in your faith, established and firm, not moved from the hope held out in the gospel. This is the gospel that you heard and that has been proclaimed to every creature under heaven, and of which I, Paul, have become a servant.

WORTHY IS THE LAMB

REVELATION 5:1-14

T hen I saw in the right hand of him who sat on the throne a scroll with writing on both sides and sealed with seven seals. And I saw a mighty angel proclaiming in a loud voice, "Who is worthy to break the seals and open the scroll?" But no one in heaven or on the earth or under the earth could open the scroll or even look inside it. I wept and wept because no one was found who was worthy to open the scroll or look inside. Then one of the elders said to me, "Do not weep! See, the Lion of the tribe of Judah, the Root of David, has triumphed. He is able to open the scroll and its seven seals."

Then I saw a Lamb, looking as if it had been slain, standing in the center of the throne, encircled by the four living creatures and the elders. He had seven horns and seven eyes, which are the seven spirits of God sent out into all the earth. He came and took the scroll from the right hand of him who sat on the throne. And when he had taken it, the four living creatures and the twenty-four elders fell down before the Lamb. Each one had a harp and they were holding golden bowls full of incense, which are the prayers of the saints. And they sang a new song:

> "You are worthy to take the scroll
> and to open its seals,
> because you were slain,
> and with your blood you purchased men for God
> from every tribe and language and people and nation.
> You have made them to be a kingdom and priests to serve our God,
> and they will reign on the earth."

Then I looked and heard the voice of many angels, numbering thousands upon thousands, and ten thousand times ten thousand. They encircled the throne and the living creatures and the elders. In a loud voice they sang:

> "Worthy is the Lamb, who was slain,
> to receive power and wealth and wisdom and strength
> and honor and glory and praise!"

Then I heard every creature in heaven and on earth and under the earth and on the sea, and all that is in them, singing:

> "To him who sits on the throne and to the Lamb
> be praise and honor and glory and power,
>   for ever and ever!"

The four living creatures said, "Amen," and the elders fell down and worshiped.

THE NEW HEAVEN AND NEW EARTH

REVELATION 21:1-7

Then I saw a new heaven and a new earth, for the first heaven and the first earth had passed away, and there was no longer any sea. I saw the Holy City, the new Jerusalem, coming down out of heaven from God, prepared as a bride beautifully dressed for her husband. And I heard a loud voice from the throne saying, "Now the dwelling of God is with men, and he will live with them. They will be his people, and God himself will be with them and be their God. He will wipe every tear from their eyes. There will be no more death or mourning or crying or pain, for the old order of things has passed away."

He who was seated on the throne said, "I am making everything new!" Then he said, "Write this down, for these words are trustworthy and true."

He said to me: "It is done. I am the Alpha and the Omega, the Beginning and the End. To him who is thirsty I will give to drink without cost from the spring of the water of life. He who overcomes will inherit all this, and I will be his God and he will be my son."

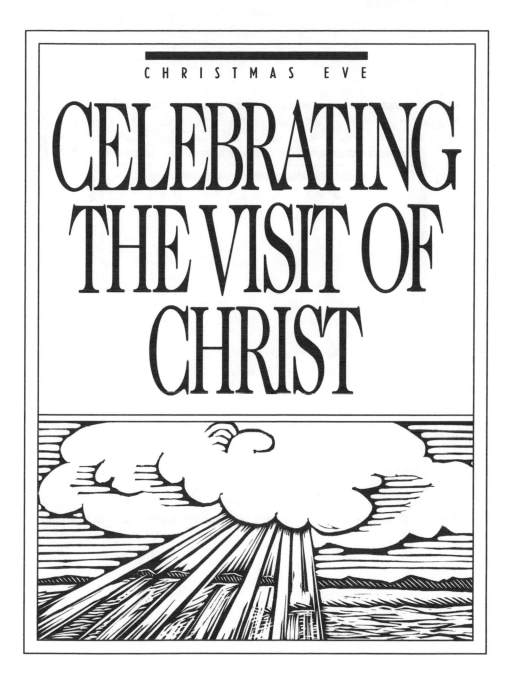

CHRISTMAS EVE

CELEBRATING THE VISIT OF CHRIST

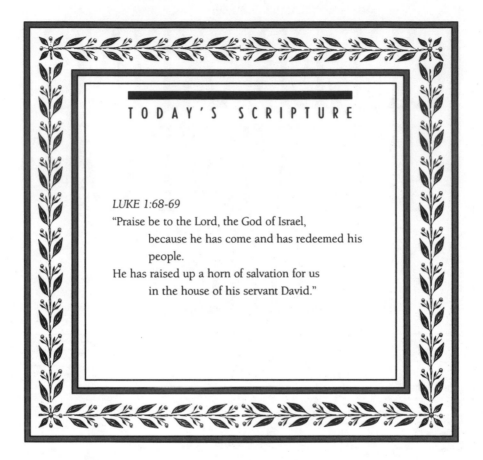

TODAY'S SCRIPTURE

LUKE 1:68-69
"Praise be to the Lord, the God of Israel,
    because he has come and has redeemed his
    people.
He has raised up a horn of salvation for us
    in the house of his servant David."

CHRISTMAS EVE

JOY TO THE WORLD

Joy to the world! the Lord is come:
Let earth receive her King;
Let every heart prepare Him room,
And heaven and nature sing, And heaven and nature sing,
And heaven, and heaven and nature sing.

Joy to the world! the Savior reigns:
Let men their songs employ;
While fields and floods, rocks, hills, and plains
Repeat the sounding joy, Repeat the sounding joy,
Repeat, repeat the sounding joy.

No more let sins and sorrows grow,
Nor thorns infest the ground;
He comes to make His blessings flow
Far as the curse is found, Far as the curse is found,
Far as, far as the curse is found.

He rules the world with truth and grace,
And makes the nations prove
The glories of His righteousness,
And wonders of His love, And wonders of His love,
And wonders, wonders of His love.

Psalm 98, Adapted by Isaac Watts
George Frederich Handel, Composer

The Bishop of Christmas

BY R.C. SPROUL

he New Testament word for *bishop* is the term *episcopus*. (We get the word *Episcopal* from it.) The word *episcopus* has a rich and fascinating history. It comes from the same word from which we get our word *scope*.

A scope is an instrument we use to look at things. We have microscopes to look at little things and telescopes to look at things that are far away. The prefix *epi* serves simply to strengthen the root.

We see then that an episcopus is a person who looks at something closely. In the ancient Greek world an episcopus could be a military general who periodically visited various units of the army to make them stand inspection. If the troops were alert, sharp, and battle-ready, they received the praise of the episcopus. If the troops were lazy and ill-prepared, they received a stinging rebuke from the episcopus.

A strange twist is found in the verb form of the Greek *episcopus*. The verb form means "to visit." The type of visit that is in view, however, is not that of a casual, drop-in appearance, but a visit that involves a careful watch of the situation. This kind of visit is by one who exercises deep care for the one he is visiting.

Bishops are called *bishops* because they are the overseers of the flock of God. They are called to visit the sick, the imprisoned, the hungry, and so on. They are given the care of the people of God.

In the Bible, the Supreme Bishop is God Himself. God has all men under His constant watch. His eye examines each one of us intensely. He numbers the very hairs of our heads and hears every word that escapes our lips.

In the Old Testament the prophets spoke of the day of the "visitation of God." It was seen sometimes as a day of great comfort and rejoicing and at other times as a day of great distress and judgment.

At the birth of Jesus, God visited the earth. The Supreme Bishop appeared in the flesh. This visitation is celebrated in the hymn of Zechariah. In his song Zechariah twice mentions God's divine visitation:

Blessed is the Lord God of Israel,

For He has visited and redeemed His people,

And has raised up a horn of salvation for us

In the house of His servant David . . .

Through the tender mercy of our God,

With which the Dayspring from on high has visited us. (Luke 1:68-69,78; NKJV)

The New Testament calls Jesus the "Bishop of our souls." He is the Bishop Incarnate. His visit to this world has changed the course of history.

The initial visit of our heavenly Bishop was cloaked in mystery. He came not as a military general, but as a baby in a rock-hewn crib. But He came to care for our souls. He came to see our situation. He came with divine blessing and redemption. He also came with a divine warning.

The Bishop of Christmas announced to the world that at some future date He would make a second visit. He promised to appear once more to review His troops. For those who love His coming, His next visit will be an occasion of unspeakable joy and glory. At that visit the fulfillment of His Bishop's task will be complete.

For those who ignore the first visit of the Bishop of Christmas, His second visit will be one of sudden disaster. That will be the Day of the Lord, the day Amos described as a day of darkness, with no light in it.

The scope of God is on each one of us. It penetrates every barrier, every mask of concealment. Our Bishop looks at us. He will not overlook us.

We long for the gaze of Jesus. We await His next visit with joyous anticipation. He cares for our souls. He visits His people to comfort and redeem. He is the Bishop of Christmas. We celebrate His wondrous visit.

QUESTIONS AND THOUGHTS

1. How do you feel knowing that Christ as Bishop is looking intensely at His world, His Church, and His people?
2. What do you think about when you consider the Second Coming (visit) of Jesus? What do you think will happen then?

FAMILY ACTIVITY

WHAT IS NEEDED:
Name of each family member on a piece of paper, folded so the name can't be seen.
Container to hold folded papers for drawing.
Paper, pencils, and/or crayons.

Read Luke 1:67-69 again.

CHRISTMAS EVE

Discuss: What gifts did Jesus give us on His first visit?

Have each person pick a name from the container (if you pick your own, return it, folded, to the container and pick again).

Prepare the gift of a drawing or brief written message for the person whose name you picked. Your gift will be a reminder of why Christ visited us.

If you haven't opened the gifts under the tree yet, do so with the prayer that gifts given and received will remind you that God has given the gift of Jesus' visit and that He will visit again.

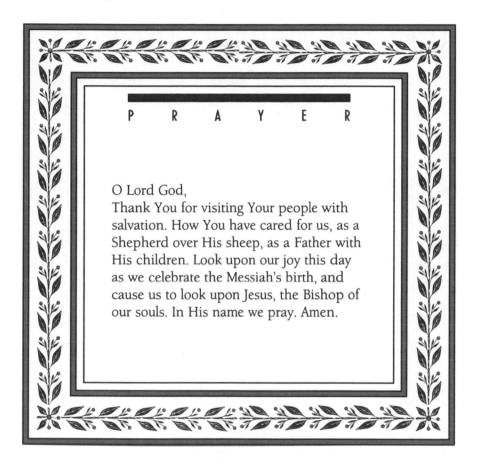

P R A Y E R

O Lord God,
Thank You for visiting Your people with salvation. How You have cared for us, as a Shepherd over His sheep, as a Father with His children. Look upon our joy this day as we celebrate the Messiah's birth, and cause us to look upon Jesus, the Bishop of our souls. In His name we pray. Amen.

HARK! THE HERALD ANGELS SING

Hark! the herald angels sing, "Glory to the newborn King:
Peace on earth, and mercy mild, God and sinners reconciled!"
Joyful, all ye nations, rise, Join the triumph of the skies;
With the angelic host proclaim, "Christ is born in Bethlehem!"
Hark! the herald angels sing, "Glory to the newborn King."

Christ, by highest heaven adored; Christ, the everlasting Lord!
Late in time behold Him come, Offspring of the Virgin's womb.
Veiled in flesh the Godhead see; Hail the incarnate Deity,
Pleased as man with men to dwell, Jesus, our Emmanuel.
Hark! the herald angels sing, "Glory to the newborn King."

Hail, the heaven-born Prince of Peace! Hail the Son of Righteousness!
Light and life to all He brings, Risen with healing in His wings.
Mild He lays His glory by, Born that man no more may die;
Born to raise the sons of earth, Born to give them second birth.
Hark! the herald angels sing, "Glory to the newborn King."

Charles Wesley, Author
Felix Mendelssohn, Composer